VOICE ★ PIANO ★ GUITAR

BEST KNOWN CHRISTMAS SONGS

W9-DBH-603

WINTER WONDERLAND

Words by
DICK SMITH

Music by
FELIX BERNARD

LITTLE SAINT NICK

Words and Music by
BRIAN WILSON

Little Saint Nick - 4 - 1

5

6

RUDOLPH THE RED-NOSED REINDEER

Words and Music by
JOHNNY MARKS

ROCKIN' AROUND THE CHRISTMAS TREE

Words and Music by
JOHNNY MARKS

CHRISTMAS AULD LANG SYNE

Words and Music by
MANN CURTIS and FRANK MILITARY

THE CHRISTMAS WALTZ

Words by
SAMMY CAHN

Music by
JULE STYNE

I'LL BE HOME FOR CHRISTMAS

Words by
KIM GANNON

Music by
WALTER KENT

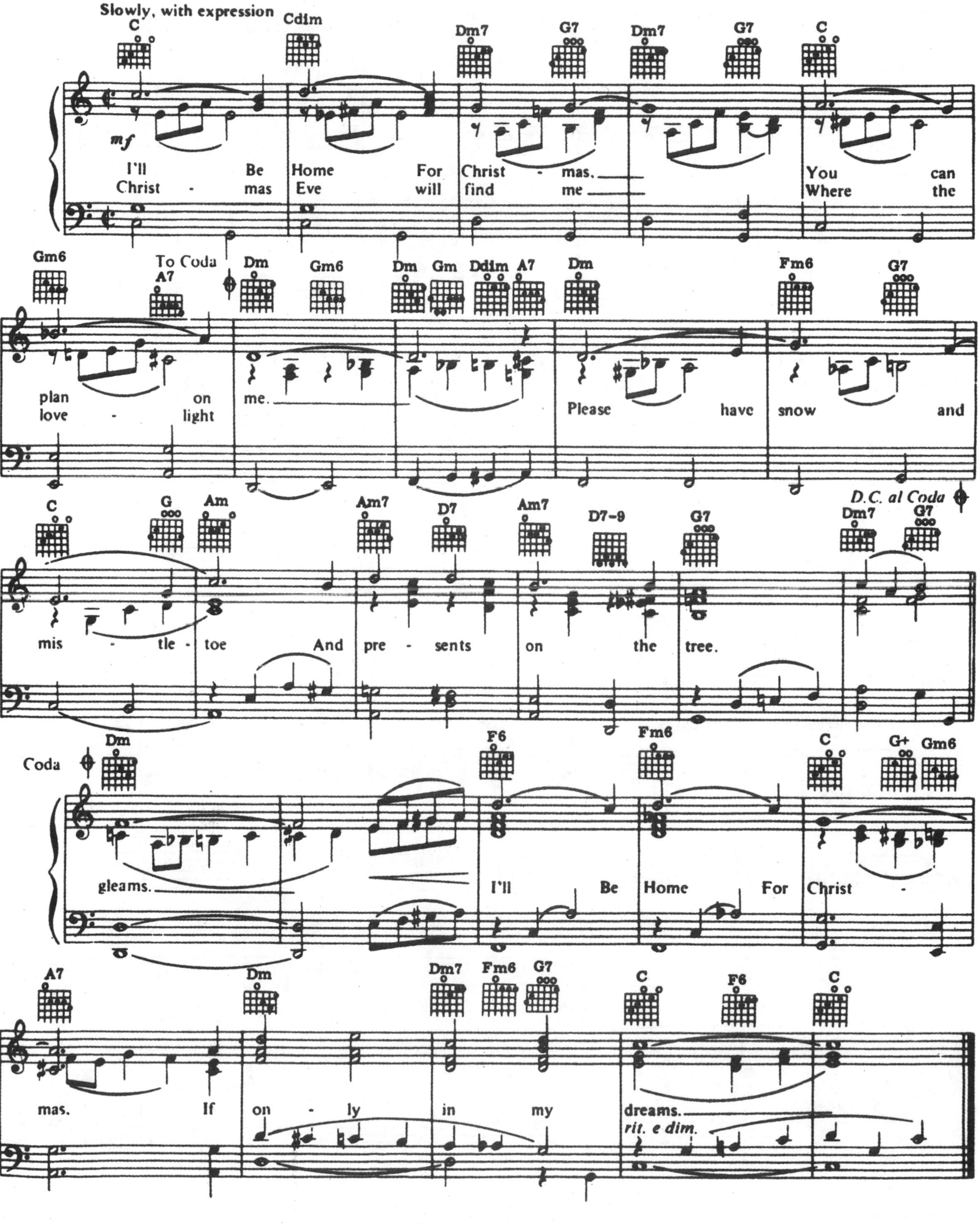

Slowly, with expression

I'll Be Home For Christ - mas. You can
Christ - mas Eve will find me Where can the

plan on me.
love - light me.
Please have snow and

mis - tle - toe And pre - sents on the tree.

Coda
gleams. I'll Be Home For Christ -

mas. If on - ly in my dreams.
rit. e dim.

ALL I WANT FOR CHRISTMAS IS
MY TWO FRONT TEETH

Words and Music by
DON GARDNER

JINGLE BELLS

Traditional

"Reproduced from THE BOOK OF HYMNS".

Deck the Halls

Traditional Welsh Melody

Words traditional

With spirit

1. Deck the halls with boughs of hol - ly,
2. See the blaz - ing Yule be - fore us,
3. Fast a - way the old year pass - es,
Fa, la, la, la, la, la, la, la, la.

Tis the sea - son to be jol - ly,
Strike the harp and join the cho - rus,
Hail the new, ye lads and lass - es,
Fa, la, la, la, la, la, la, la, la.

Don we now our gay ap - par - el,
Fol - low me in mer - ry meas - ure,
Sing we joy - ous all to - geth - er,
Fa, la, la, la, la, la, la, la, la.

Troll the an - cient Yule - tide car - ol,
While I tell of Yule - tide treas - ure,
Heed - less of the wind and weath - er,
Fa, la, la, la, la, la, la, la, la.

19

SILENT NIGHT

Words by
JOSEPH MOHR

Music by
FRANZ GRUBER

Calmly with reverence

1. Si - lent night! Ho - ly night! All is calm, all is bright.
2. Si - lent night! Ho - ly night! Shep - herds quake at the sight!
3. Si - lent night! Ho - ly night! Son of God, love's pure light!

Round yon Vir - gin Moth - er and Child! Ho - ly In - fant, so ten - der and mild,
Glo - ries stream from heav - en a - far, Heav'n - ly hosts sing, "Al - le - lu - ia!"
Ra - diant beams from Thy ho - ly face With the dawn of re - deem - ing grace,

Sleep in heav - en - ly peace! Sleep in heav - en - ly peace!
Christ, the Sav - ior, is born! Christ, the Sav - ior, is born!
Je - sus, Lord, at Thy birth! Je - sus, Lord, at Thy birth!

AWAY IN A MANGER

by
MARTIN LUTHER

CHRISTMAS ALPHABET

Words and Music by
BUDDY KAYE and JULES LOMAN

Chorus (*Moderato Slow*)

"C" is for the Can-dy trimmed a-round the Christ-mas tree.

"H" is for the Hap-pi-ness with all the fam-i-ly. "R" is for the Rein-deer pranc-ing

by the win-dow pane. "I" is for the Ic-ing on the

Christmas Alphabet - 2 - 1

HAVE YOURSELF A MERRY LITTLE CHRISTMAS

Words and Music by
HUGH MARTIN and
RALPH BLANE

Have Yourself a Merry Little Christmas - 3 - 1

28

JOY TO THE WORLD

Words by
ISAAC WATTS

Music by
GEORGE F. HANDEL

Maestoso

1. Joy to the world! the Lord has come: Let earth re-ceive her King; Let
2. Joy to the world! the Sav-ior reigns: Let men their songs em-ploy, While
3. No more let sin and sor-row grow, Nor thorns in-fest the ground; He
4. He rules the world with truth and grace, And makes the na-tion prove The

ev-'ry heart pre-pare Him room, And heav'n and na-ture sing And
fields and floods, rocks, hills and plains, Re-peat the sound-ing joy, Re-
comes to make His bless-ings flow Far as the curse is found Far
glo-ries of His right-eous-ness And won-ders of His love, And

And heav'n and na-ture

heav'n and na-ture sing, And heav'n, and heav'n and na-ture sing.
peat the sound-ing joy, Re-peat, re-peat the sound-ing joy.
as the curse is found, Far as, far as the curse is found.
won-ders of His love, And won-ders, won-ders of His love.

sing. And heav'n and na-ture sing,

TOYLAND

Words by
GLEN MAC DONOUGH

Music by
VICTOR HERBERT

roll so swift - ly by_____ And of the man - y
first pale gleam of gray._____ Then of the past you'll

p animato e cresc.

lands_____ You will have jour - neyed through____ You'll
dream____ As gray - haired grown ups do_____ And

oft re - call The best of all, The land your child - hood
seek once more Its phan - tom shore, The land your child - hood

molto rit.

knew! _____ Your child - hood knew.
knew! _____ Your child - hood knew.

mf   *molto rit. e dim.*   *p*

SANTA BABY

Words and Music by
JOAN JAVITS, PHIL SPRINGER
and TONY SPRINGER

Mis-ter "Claus," I feel as tho I know ya ___ So you won't mind if I should get fam-

mil - ya, will ya? San - ta Ba - by, just slip a sa - ble un - der the tree ___
San - ta Ba - by, one lit - tle thing I real - ly do need; ___

___ for me. ___ Been an aw - ful good girl ___ San - ta Ba - by, So
___ The deed ___ to a pla - tin - um mine ___ San - ta hon - ey, So

BUON NATALE
(Means Merry Christmas To You)

Words and Music by
BOB SAFFER and FRANK LINALE

WE WISH YOU A MERRY CHRISTMAS

Traditional English Folk Song

O HOLY NIGHT

Words and Music by
ADOLPHE ADAM

THE TWELVE DAYS OF CHRISTMAS

Old English

44

6. On the___ sixth___ day of Christ-mas, my true love gave to me,
7. On the___ sev-enth day of Christ-mas, my true love gave to me,
8. On the___ eighth___ day of Christ-mas, my true love gave to me,
9. On the___ ninth___ day of Christ-mas, my true love gave to me,
10. On the___ tenth___ day of Christ-mas, my true love gave to me,
11. On the e-lev-enth day of Christ-mas, my true love gave to me,   E-
12. On the___ twelfth___ day of Christ-mas, my true love gave to me,

6th VERSE   **To Refrain**   **7th VERSE**   **To Refrain**

Six geese a - lay - ing,   Sev - en swans a - swim-ming, Six geese a - lay-ing,

* VERSES 8, 9, 10, 11, 12   **To Refrain**

8. Eight___ maids a - milk-ing,   Sev-en swans a swim-ming, Six geese a - lay-ing.
9. Nine___ la - dies wait-ing,
10. Ten___ lords a - leap-ing,
11. lev - en pip-ers pip-ing,
12. Twelve_ drum-mers drum-ming.

***This measure to be repeated as often as necessary, so that text may be
sung in inverse order, ending each time with "Eight maids a-milking".**

O LITTLE TOWN OF BETHLEHEM

Words by
PHILLIPS BROOKS

Music by
LEWIS H. REDNER

A CHILD THIS DAY IS BORN

Traditional - English

1. A Child this day is born, A Child of high re-nown; Most worthy of a scep-tre, A scep-tre and a crown.
2. These tid-ings shep-herds heard, Whilst watch-ing o'er their fold; 'Twas by an An-gel un-to them. That night re-vealed and told.

Glad ti-dings to all men, Glad ti-dings sing we may, Be-cause the King of Kings Was born on Christ-mas Day!

ANGELS WE HAVE HEARD ON HIGH

(Westminster Carol)

Traditional French - English

1. An - gels we have heard on high, Sweet - ly sing - ing o'er the plains;
2. Shep - herds, why this ju - bi - lee? Why your joy - ous songs pro - long?
3. Come to Beth - le - hem and see Him whose birth the an - gels sing;

And the moun - tains in re - ply Ech - o - ing their joy - ous strains.
What the glad - some ti - dings be Which in - spire your heav'n - ly song? Glo -
Come a - dore on bend - ed knee Christ, the Lord, our new - born King.

- ri - a in ex - cel - sis De - o, Glo -

- ri - a in ex - cel - sis De - o!

ANGELS FROM THE REALMS OF GLORY

Words by
JAMES MONTGOMERY

Music by
HENRY SMART

O COME ALL YE FAITHFUL
(Adeste Fidelis)

By
JOHN FRANCIS WADE

IT DOESN'T HAVE TO BE THAT WAY

Words and Music by
JIM CROCE

53

(There's No Place Like)
HOME FOR THE HOLIDAYS

Words by
AL STILLMAN

Music by
ROBERT ALLEN

57

A HOLLY JOLLY CHRISTMAS

Words and Music by
JOHNNY MARKS

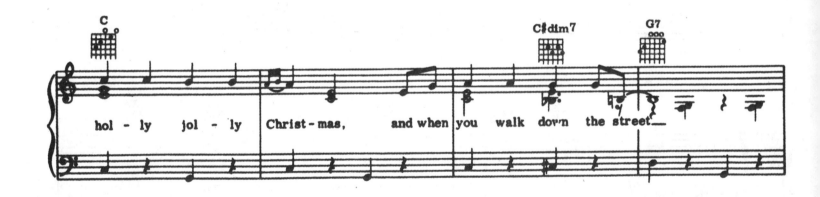

I HEARD THE BELLS ON CHRISTMAS DAY

Words by
HENRY WADSWORTH LONGFELLOW
(Adapted by John Marks)

Music by
JOHN MARKS

GOOD KING WENCESLAS

Words by
JOHN NEAL

Music Traditional

Moderato

1. Good King Wen-ces-las look'd out On the feast of Ste-phen When the snow lay
2. "Hith-er, page, and stand by me, If thou know'st it, tell-ing Yon-der peas-ant,
3. "Bring me flesh and bring me wine, Bring me pine-logs hith-er; Thou and I will
4. "Sire, the night is dark-er now, And the wind blows strong-er Fails my heart, I

round a-bout, Deep and crisp and e-ven; Bright-ly shone the moon that night,
who is he? Where, and what his dwell-ing?" "Sire, he lives a good league hence,
see him dine When we bear them thith-er." Page and mon-arch forth they went.
know not how, I can go no long-er." Mark my foot-steps, my good page,

Tho' the frost was cru-el, When a poor man came in sight Gath-'ring win-ter fu - el.
Un-der-neath the moun-tain; Right a-gainst the for-est fence, By Saint Ag-nes' foun-tain."
Forth they went to-geth-er, Thro' the rude wind's wild la-ment And the bit-ter weath-er.
Tread, thou in them bold-ly: Thou shalt find the win-ter's rage Freeze thy blood-less cold - ly."

I BELIEVE

Words and Music by
ERVIN DRAKE, IRVIN GRAHAM,
JIMMY SHIRL and AL STILLMAN

COLOR THE CHILDREN

Words and Music by
E. G. SCHWEIKERT

* Alternate lyrics suitable for Christmas.

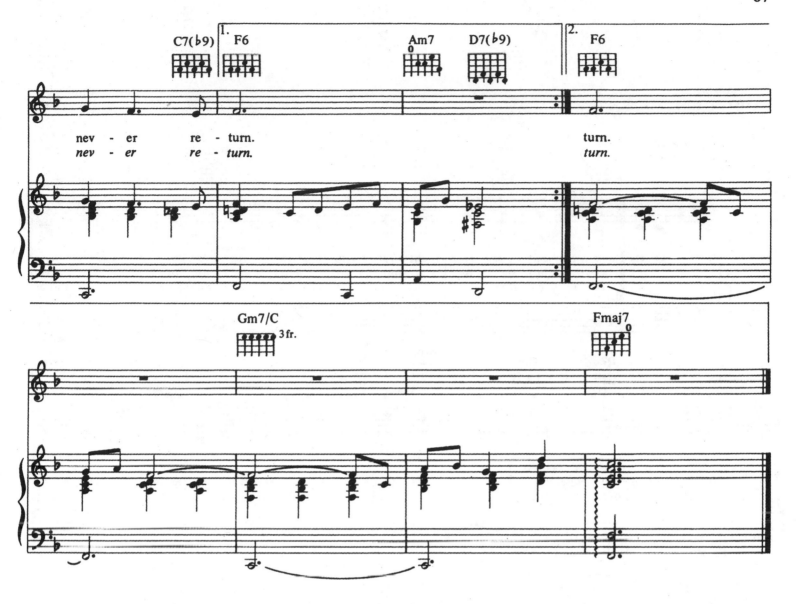

2nd Chorus

Color the children With summer-time greens, Bright Easter baskets And pink jelly beans.	*Color the children* *With mistletoe green,* *Kisses below it,* *Laughs in between.*
Color them stories They like to be told, Galleons and pirates And treasures of gold.	*Color them cookies* *That Grandmother made.* *Santa ho-hoing* *In Macy's Parade.*
Color the children With daydreams and song, Lands of adventure Where children belong.	*Color the children* *An old memory,* *Rainbows of color* *To light up the tree.*
And color them rainbows Of love and concern, For once they're gone They'll never return.	*Color them Christmas* *With love and concern,* *For once they are gone* *They'll never return.*

LET IT SNOW! LET IT SNOW! LET IT SNOW!

Words by
SAMMY CAHN

Music by
JULE STYNE

O CHRISTMAS TREE
(O TANNENBAUM)

German Folk Song

* **Repeat words as well as music of first four measures.**

GO TELL IT ON THE MOUNTAIN

Negro Christmas Spiritual

1. When I was a learn-er I sought both night and day, I
2. He made me a watch-man up-on the cit-y wall An'

asked the Lord to aid me and He show'd me the way. _____
if I am a Chris-tian I am the least of all. _____

Go tell it on the moun-tains, O-ver the hills an' ev-'ry-where,

Go tell it on the moun-tains, Our Je-sus Christ is born.

COME, SHEPHERDS, RISE!

Bohemian Carol, VI Century
English Version by
F.C.W.

ALMOST DAY (IT'S ALMOST DAY)

Words and Music by
HUDDIE LEDBETTER

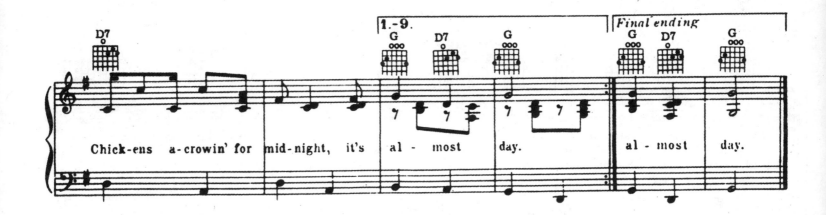

2. Santa Claus is coming,
   It's almost day;
   Santa Claus is coming,
   It's almost day.

3. Candy canes and sugar plums,
   On Christmas day;
   Candy canes and sugar plums,
   On Christmas day.

4. Mama 'll stuff a turkey
   On Christmas day;
   Mama 'll stuff a turkey
   On Christmas day.

5. Quit your peeping 'round the corner,
   It's almost day;
   Quit your peeping 'round the corner,
   It's almost day.

6. Hang your stockings on the chimney
   For Christmas day;
   Hang your stockings on the chimney
   For Christmas day.

7. I want a size fifty stocking
   For Christmas day;
   I want a size fifty stocking
   For Christmas day.

8. Santa Claus is coming
   On Christmas day;
   Santa Claus is coming
   On Christmas day.

9. Chickens a-crowing for midnight,
   It's almost day;
   Chickens a-crowing for midnight,
   It's almost day.

BESIDE THY MANGER HERE I STAND

"Vom Himmel Hoch"
MARTIN LUTHER

1. Be - side Thy man - ger here I stand, Dear
2. With joy I gaze___ up - on Thy face, Thy

Je - su Lord, and Sav - ior, A gift of love___ with -
glo - ry and Thy splen - dor Are great - er than___ my

in my hand To thank Thee for Thy___ fa - vor.
heart can praise, And songs can fit - ly___ ren - der.

GATHER AROUND THE CHRISTMAS TREE

By JOHN HOPKINS

Moderately

Gath-er a-round the Christ-mas tree! Gath-er a-round the Christ-mas tree!

1. Ev - er green have its branch-es been, It is king of all the wood-land scene; For
2. Once the pride of the moun-tain side, Now cut down to grace our Christ-mas-tide: For
3. Ev - 'ry bough has a bur-den now, They are gifts of love for us, we trow: For

Christ, our King, is born to-day! His reign shall nev-er pass a-way.
Christ from heav'n to earth came down, To gain, through death, a nob-ler crown.
Christ is born, His love to show, And give good gifts to men be-low.

CHORUS

Ho - san - na, Ho - san - na, Ho - san - na in the high - est!

THE CHRISTMAS CHILD
Quand Dieu naquit a Noel

A French Noël
Harmonized and set by
Douglas Mac Lean

BURGUNDIAN CAROL

Words by
OSCAR BRAND

Music by
PAUL CAMPBELL

2. And on that night it has been told,
These humble beasts so rough and rude,
Throughout the night of holy birth,
Drank no water, ate no food.
How many oxen and donkeys now,
Dressed in ermine, silk and such,
How many oxen and donkeys you know
At such a time would do as much?

3. As soon as to these humble beasts
Appeared our Lord, so mild and sweet,
With joy they knelt before His grace,
And gently kissed His tiny feet.
If we, like oxen and donkeys then,
In spite of all the things we've heard,
Would be like oxen and donkeys then,
We'd hear the truth, believe His word.

JOLLY OLD SAINT NICHOLAS

I'LL WALK WITH GOD

Words by
PAUL FRANCIS WEBSTER

Music by
NICHOLAS BRODSZKY

Moderately, with deep emotion

I FOUND THE ANSWER

Words and Music by
JOHNNY LANGE (ASCAP)

Chorus

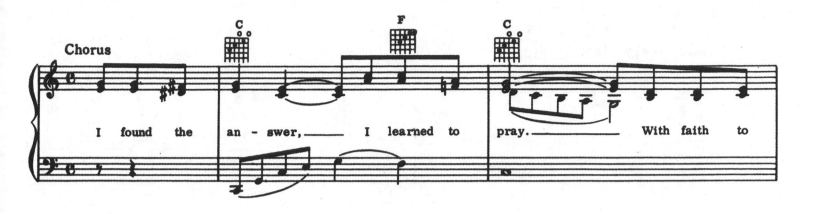

I found the an - swer,_____ I learned to pray._____ With faith to

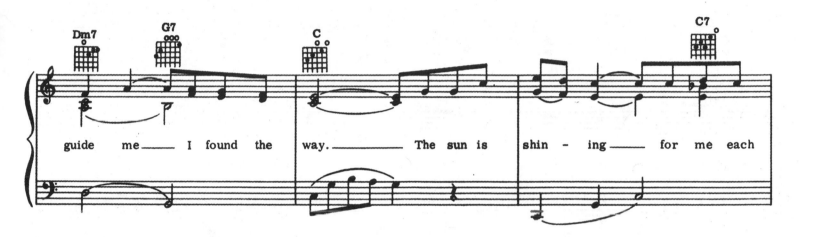

guide me_____ I found the way._____ The sun is shin - ing_____ for me each

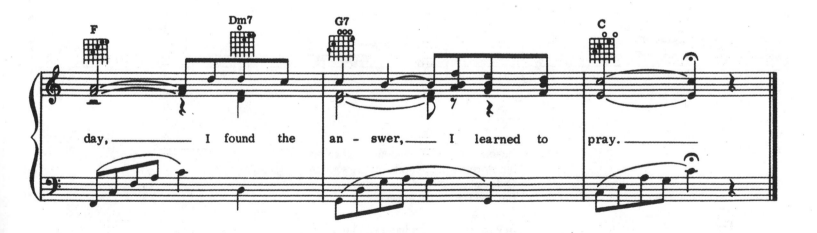

day,_____ I found the an - swer,_____ I learned to pray._____

2. I was sad and lonely, all my hopes were gone,
   Days were long and dreary, I couldn't carry on.
   Then I found the courage to keep my head up high,
   Once again I'm happy and here's the reason why.

   Chorus

3. Keep your Bible with you. read it ev'ry day,
   Always count your blessings and always stop to pray.
   Learn to keep believing and faith will see you through,
   Seek to know contentment and it will come to you.

   Chorus

BEYOND THE SUNSET

Words by
VIRGIL P. BROCK

Music by
BLANCHE KERR BROCK

2. Beyond the sunset no clouds will gather,
   No storms will threaten, no fears annoy;
   O day of gladness, O day unended,
   Beyond the sunset, eternal joy!

3. Beyond the sunset a hand will guide me
   To God, the Father, whom I adore;
   His glorious presence, His words of welcome,
   Will be my portion on that fair shore.

4. Beyond the sunset, O glad reunion,
   With our dear loved ones who've gone before;
   In that fair homeland we'll know no parting,
   Beyond the sunset forever-more!

GOOD CHRISTIAN MEN, REJOICE

Words by
JOHN NEALE

Music Old German

HAPPY BIRTHDAY, JESUS

Words by
ESTELLE LEVITT

Music by
LEE POCKRISS

1. Ka - ty got a dol - ly that cries and blinks its eyes;
2. Ted - dy bears get bro - ken, and trains will rust a - way;
3. Chris - mas is for chil - dren and now I have my own; Their

Jim - my got an au - to - mat - ic plane that real - ly flies. But
All the fan - cy play - things seem to fall a - part one day. But
eyes are full of won - der when all the toys are shown. But I'll

87

THE STAR CAROL

Words by
WIHLA HUTSON

Music by
ALFRED BURT

1. Long years a - go on a deep win - ter night,
2. Je - sus, the Lord was that Ba - by so small,
3. Dear Ba - by Je - sus, how ti - ny Thou art,

High in the heav'ns a star shone bright,
Laid down to sleep in a hum - ble stall;
I'll make a place for Thee in my heart,

While in a man - ger a wee in - fant lay,
Then came the star and it stood o - ver - head,
And when the stars in the heav - ens I see,

Sweet - ly a - sleep on a bed of hay.
Shed - ding its light 'round His lit - tle bed.
Ev - er and al - ways I think of Thee.

WE THREE KINGS OF ORIENT ARE

THERE IS NO CHRISTMAS LIKE A HOME CHRISTMAS

Words by
CARL SIGMAN

Music by
MICKEY J. ADDY

OUT OF THE EAST

Words and Music by
HARRY NOBLE

1. Out of the East there came rid - ing, rid - ing, Three of the wis - est of men,
2. In - to the West they went rid - ing, rid - ing, Fol - low-ing af - ter the star,
3. Low in a man - ger they found Him, found Him, Bathed in the light of yon star,

SLEEP, HOLY BABE

Words by
EDWARD CASWALL

Music by
JOHN B. DYKES

THE ONLY THING I WANT FOR CHRISTMAS

By
VICK KNIGHT, JOHNNY LANGE
and LEW PORTER

UP ON THE HOUSE TOP

Traditional

I DON'T WANT A LOT FOR CHRISTMAS

Words and Music by
MILTON PASCAL and GERALD MARKS

IN THE GARDEN

Words and Music by
C. AUSTIN MILES

2. He speaks, and the sound of His voice
   Is so sweet, the birds hush their singing,
   And the melody,
   That He gave to me,
   Within my heart is ringing.

   Chorus

3. I'd stay in the garden with Him,
   Tho' the night around me be falling,
   But He bids me go;
   Thro' the voice of woe,
   His voice to me is calling.

   Chorus

HE'S ONLY A PRAYER AWAY

Words and Music by
JOHNNY LANGE and HAROLD L. GRAHAM
ASCAP   ASCAP

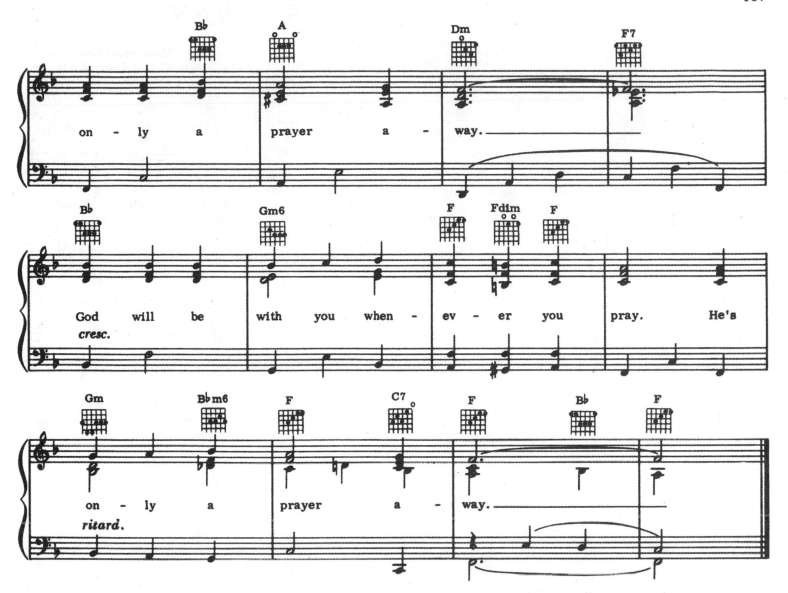

2. Though friends may deride and forsake you,
   And leave you alone in the way,
   Remember the promise of Jesus,
   He's only a prayer away.

   Chorus

3. Our Lord suffered death for transgression,
   The death that each mortal should pay,
   Oh, why do you languish in sorrow,
   He's only a prayer away.

   Chorus

4. When others forsake and desert you,
   And you're in the depth of despair,
   Let God share your burden and sorrow,
   Just seek Him and He'll be there.

   Chorus

5. Though you walk alone in the darkness,
   You're lost and there's nothin' in sight,
   He's with you each step of the journey,
   He's there with His guiding light.

   Chorus

6. You followed the path of a sinner
   Temptation had led you astray,
   Remember He'll always forgive you,
   If you'll only meet Him halfway.

   Chorus

7. He has an infinite power,
   And so many things He can do,
   He'll always be ready to help you,
   Just ask Him to come to you.

   Chorus

8. Whenever you feel sad and lonely,
   'Cause all of your hopes fell apart,
   He'll bring you a new life if only,
   You'll keep Him within your heart.

   Chorus

WHAT LOVELY INFANT CAN THIS BE?

Austrian Folk Carol
Arranged by
DOUGLAS MACLEAN

1. What love-ly in-fant can this be? That in the lit-tle crib I see? So sweet-ly on the straw it lies, It must have come from Par-a-dise.
2. Who are those peo-ple kneel-ing down, With crook-ed sticks, and hands so brown? The shep-herds on the moun-tain top, The lit-tle an-gels woke them up.
3. Hail, ho-ly cave! though dark thou be, The world is light-ed up from thee. Hail, Ho-ly Babe! cre-a-tion stands And moves up-on thy ti-ny hands.

THE SEVEN JOYS OF MARY

Traditional Old English Arr. by
Sir John Stainer

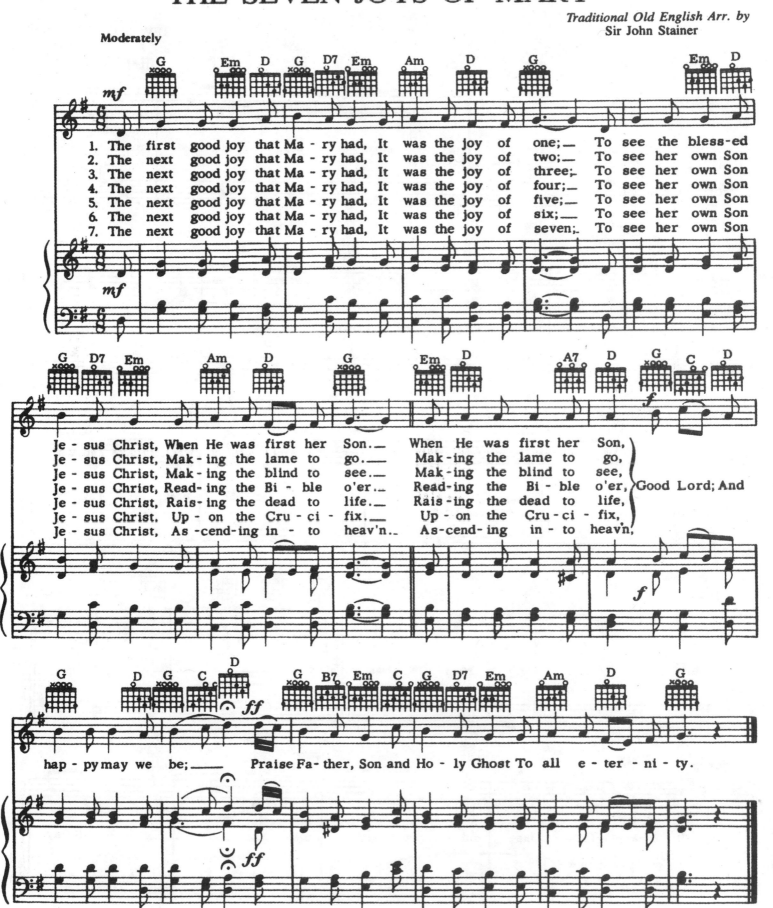

THE OLD RUGGED CROSS

Words and Music by
REV. GEO BENNARD

2. Oh that old rugged cross, so despised by the world.
   Has a wondrous attraction for me,
   For the dear Lamb of God left His glory above,
   To bear it to dark calvary.

   Chorus

3. In the old rugged cross, stained with blood so divine,
   A wondrous beauty I see.
   For 'twas on that old cross Jesus suffered and died
   To pardon and sanctify me.

   Chorus

4. To the old rugged cross, I will ever be true,
   Its shame and reproach gladly bear,
   Then He'll call on some day to my home far away,
   Where His glory forever I'll share.

   Chorus

SOMEBODY BIGGER THAN YOU AND I

Words and Music by
JOHNNY LANGE, SONNY BURKE
and HY HEATH

WHEN IT'S CHRISTMAS ON THE RANGE

By
CHARLIE TOBIAS, NAT SIMON
and ROY NEWELL

THE WHITE WORLD OF WINTER

Words by
MITCHELL PARISH

Music by
HOAGY CARMICHAEL

IT CAME UPON THE MIDNIGHT CLEAR

Words by
EDMOND H. SEARS

Music by
RICHARD S. WILLIS

1. It came up-on the mid-night clear, That glo-rious song of
2. Still thro' the clo-ven skies they came, With peace-ful wings un-
3. O ye, be-neath life's crush-ing load, Whose forms are bend-ing
4. For lo! the days are has-t'ning on, By proph-ets seen of

old,__ From an-gels bend-ing near the earth To touch their harps of
furl'd.__ And still their heav'n-ly mu-sic floats O'er all the wea-ry
low,__ Who toil a-long the climb-ing way With pain-ful steps and
old,__ When with the ev-er cir-cling years, Shall come the time fore-

gold__ "Peace on the earth,__ good will to men, From heav'ns all gra-cious
world.__ A-bove its sad__ and low-ly plains They bend on hov-'ring
slow,__ Look now, for glad__ and gold-en hours Come swift-ly on__ the
told,__ When the new heav'n. and earth shall own The Prince__ of Peace their

King." The world in sol - emn still - ness lay To hear the an - gels sing.
wing, And ev - er o'er its Ba - bel sounds The bless - ed an - gels sing.
wing, O rest be - side the wea - ry road And hear the an - gels sing.
King, And the whole world send back the song Which now the an - gels sing.

STAR OF THE EAST

Words by
GEORGE COOPER

Music by
AMANDA KENNEDY
Traditional English

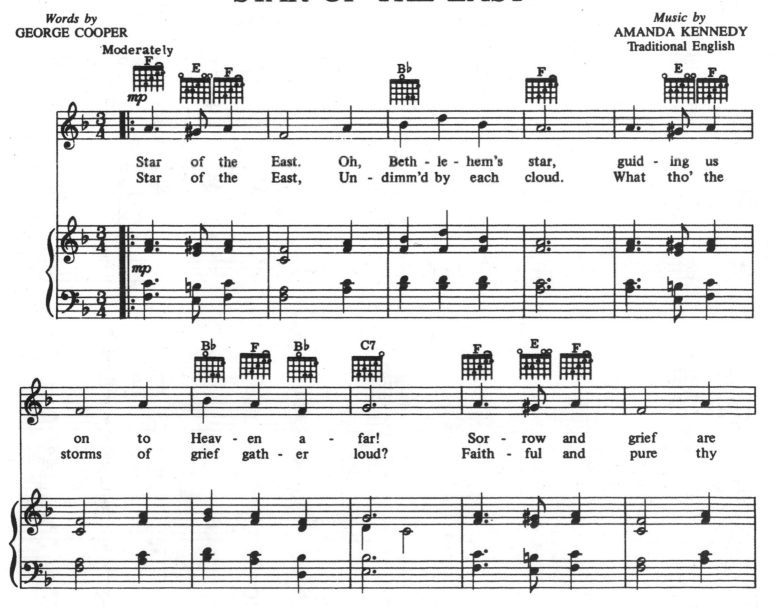

Star of the East. Oh, Beth - le - hem's star, guid - ing us
Star of the East, Un - dimm'd by each cloud. What tho' the

on to Heav - en a - far! Sor - row and grief are
storms of grief gath - er loud? Faith - ful and pure thy

DECK THE HALLS

Old Welsh

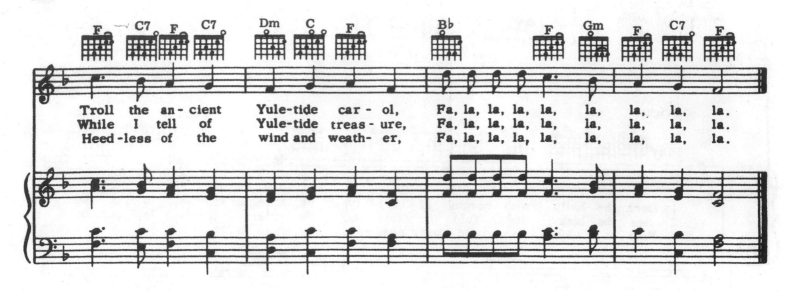

Troll the an-cient Yule-tide car-ol, Fa, la, la, la, la, la, la, la, la.
While I tell of Yule-tide treas-ure, Fa, la, la, la, la, la, la, la, la.
Heed-less of the wind and weath-er, Fa, la, la, la, la, la, la, la, la.

THE FIRST NOWELL

Traditional

Moderately

1. The first Now-ell the an-gel did say Was to
2. They look-ed up and saw a star Shin-ing
3. This star drew nigh to the north-west, O'er
4. Then en-ter'd in those wise men three, Full

cer-tain poor shep-herds in fields as they lay; In fields where they lay
in the East, be-yond them far, And to the earth it
Beth-le-hem it took its rest, And there it did both
rev-'rent-ly up-on their knee, And of-fer'd there, in

keep-ing their sheep, On a cold win-ter's night_ that was_ so deep.
gave_ great light, And_ so it con - tin - ued both day_ and night.
stop_ and stay Right_ o - ver the place_ where Je - sus lay.
His_ pres - ence, Their_ gold_ and myrrh_ and frank - in - cense.

Now - ell,_ Now - ell, Now - ell, Now - ell, Born is the King_ of Is - ra - el.

GOD REST YOU MERRY, GENTLEMEN

TRADITIONAL

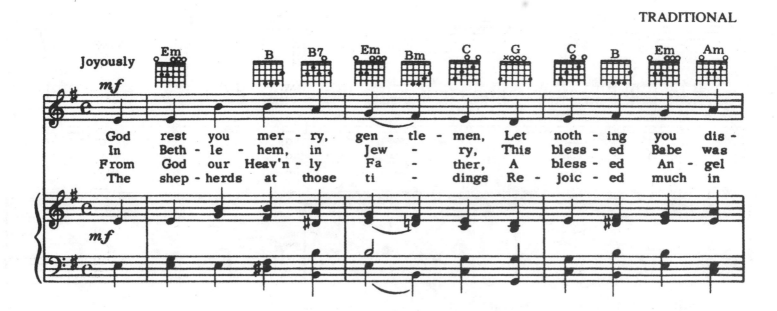

God rest you mer - ry, gen - tle - men, Let noth - ing you dis -
In Beth - le - hem, in Jew - ry, This bless - ed Babe was
From God our Heav'n - ly Fa - ther, A bless - ed An - gel
The shep - herds at those ti - dings Re - joic - ed much in

THE BABE OF BETHLEHEM

Traditional
Anonymous

1. The Babe in Beth-l'hem's man-ger laid, In hum-ble
2. A Sav-ior! sin-ners all a-round, Sing, shout the
3. For not to sit on Da-vid's throne, With world-ly
4. Well may we sing a Sav-ior's birth, Who need the

form so low; By won-d'ring an-gels is sur-vey'd Thro' all His scenes of woe.
won-drous word;Let ev-'ry bo-som hail the sound, A Sav-ior! Christ the Lord.
pomp and joy, He came for sin-ners to a-tone And Sa-tan to de-stroy.
grace so giv'n, And hail His com-ing down to earth, Who rais-es us to heav'n.

REFRAIN

No - ël, No - ël, Now sing the Sav-ior giv'n, All

hail His com-ing down to earth, Who rais-es us to heav'n.

A VIRGIN UNSPOTTED

Traditional English

REFRAIN

Dm Gm7 F Gm F Gm C G7 F G7

Aye and there - fore be mer - ry, set sor - row a -

C Dm F Bb Gm F C F Bb C7 F

side, Christ Je - sus, our Sav - ior, was born on this tide.

GLAD CHRISTMAS BELLS

Moderately

Traditional

G D D7 G Am

1. Glad Christ - mas bells, your mu - sic tells The sweet and pleas - ant
2. No pal - ace hall its ceil - ing tall His king - ly head spread
3. Nor rai - ment gay, as there He lay, A - dorn'd the in - fant
4. But from a - far, a splen - did star The wise men west - ward

D7 G D D7 G C G Am7 G D7 G

sto - ry; How came to earth, in low - ly birth, The Lord of life and glo - ry.
o - ver, There on - ly stood a sta - ble rude The heav - en - ly Babe to cov - er.
stran - ger; Poor, hum - ble Child of moth - er mild, She laid Him in a man - ger.
turn - ing; The live - long night saw pure and bright, A - bove His birth - place burn - ing.

HARK! THE HERALD ANGELS SING

Words by
CHARLES WESLEY

Music by
FELIX MENDELSSOHN

Expressively

1. Hark! the her - ald an - gels sing,__ "Glo - ry to the new-born King!
2. Christ, by high - est heav'n a - dored;__ Christ the ev - er - last-ing Lord;
3. Hail! the heav'n born Prince of Peace!__ Hail! the Son of Right-eous-ness!

Peace on earth, and mer - cy mild,__ God and sin - ners re - con-ciled." Joy - ful, all ye
Late in time be-hold him come,__ Off - spring of the fa - vored one. Veiled in flesh, the
Light and life to all he brings,__ Ris'n with heal - ing in His wings. Mild He lays His

na - tions rise,__ Join the tri - umph of the skies;__ With th'an-gel - ic host pro - claim,
God - head see;__ Hail th'in-car - nate De - i - ty__ Pleased, as man with men to dwell,
glo - ry by,__ Born that man no more may die:__ Born to raise the sons of earth,

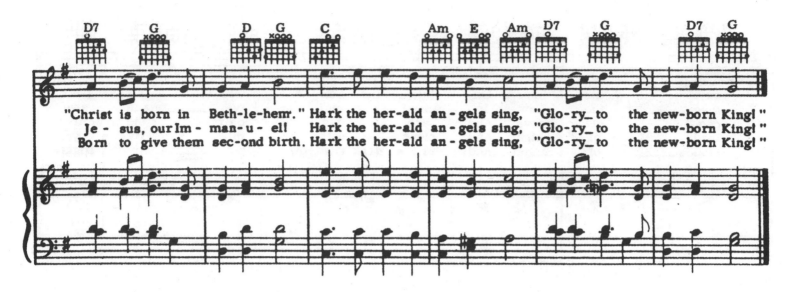

"Christ is born in Beth-le-hem." Hark the her-ald an-gels sing, "Glo-ry_ to the new-born King!"
Je - sus, our Im - man-u - ell Hark the her-ald an-gels sing, "Glo-ry_ to the new-born King!"
Born to give them sec-ond birth. Hark the her-ald an-gels sing, "Glo-ry_ to the new-born King!"

O COME, O COME, EMMANUEL

Slowly

1. O come, O come, Im - man - u - el, And
2. O come, O come, Thou Lord of might, Who
3. O come, Thou Rod of Jes - se, free, Thine
4. O come, Thou Key of Da - vid, come, And
5. O come, Thou Day - Spring, come and cheer Our

ran - som cap - tive Is - ra - el, That mourns in lone - ly
to Thy tribes, on Si - nai's height, In an - cient times did'st
own from Sa - tan's tyr - an - ny; From depths of hell thy
o - pen wide our heav'n - ly home; Make safe the way that
spir - its by Thine ad - vent here; Dis - perse the gloom - y

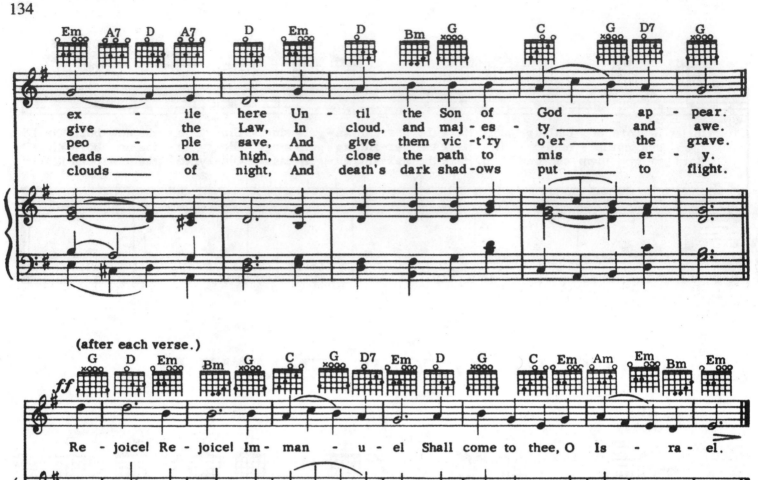

ex - ile here Un - til the Son of God _____ ap - pear.
give _____ the Law, In cloud, and maj - es - ty _____ and awe.
peo - ple save, And give them vic -t'ry o'er _____ the grave.
leads _____ on high, And close the path to mis - er - y.
clouds _____ of night, And death's dark shad -ows put _____ to flight.

(after each verse.)

Re - joice! Re - joice! Im - man - u - el Shall come to thee, O Is - ra - el.

WHAT CHILD IS THIS?
(GREENSLEEVES)

Traditional

Moderately

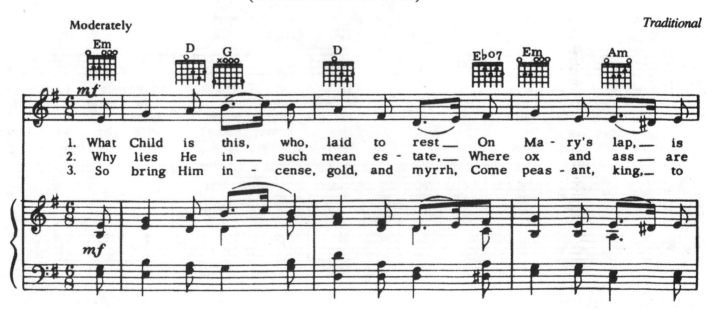

1. What Child is this, who, laid to rest___ On Ma - ry's lap,___ is
2. Why lies He in___ such mean es - tate,___ Where ox and ass___ are
3. So bring Him in - cense, gold, and myrrh, Come peas - ant, king,___ to

NOËL, NOËL

French-English
Arranged by
SIR JOHN STAINER

Cantabile

1. 'Tis the day, the bless-ed day, On which our Lord was born,__ And sweet-ly do the sun-beams gild The dew__ be-span-gled thorn.__ The birds sing through the heav-ens clear, The breez-es gent-ly play,__ And song and sun-shine love-ly, Be-gin__ this Ho-ly Day.__

2. In a hum-ble feed-ing trough, With-in a low-ly shed,__ With cat-tle at His in-fant feet, And shep-herds at His head,__ The Sav-ior of this sin-ful world In in-no-cence first lay,__ And wise men made their off-'ring, Up-on__ a Ho-ly Day.__

3. He will save the per-ish-ing, Will waft the sighs to heav'n,__ Of guilt-y men, who tru-ly seek, And weep__ to be for-giv'n__ And In-ter-ces-sor still He shines, And men to Him should pray,__ Be-fore His al-tar meek-ly, Up-on__ this Ho-ly Day.__

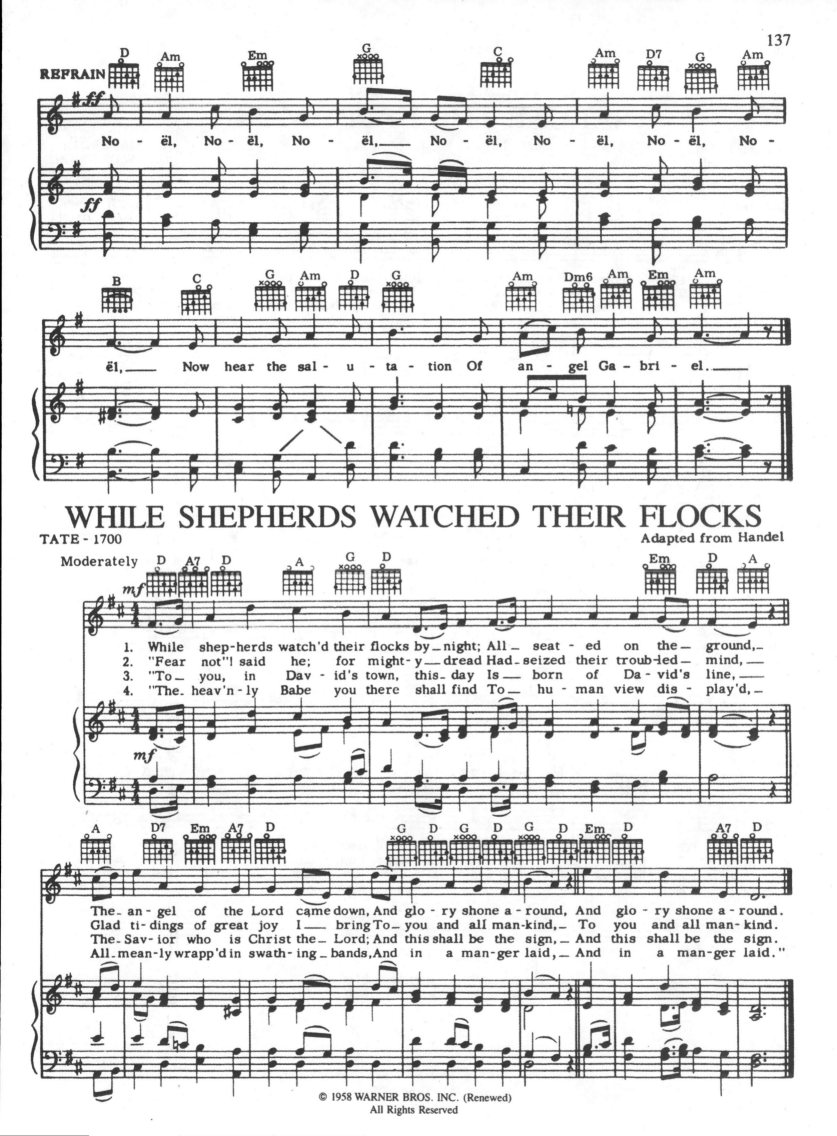

WHILE SHEPHERDS WATCHED THEIR FLOCKS

TATE - 1700

Adapted from Handel

Moderately

1. While shep-herds watch'd their flocks by night; All seat - ed on the ground,
2. "Fear not"I said he; for might-y dread Had seized their troub-led mind,
3. "To you, in Dav - id's town, this day Is born of Da - vid's line,
4. "The heav'n-ly Babe you there shall find To hu - man view dis - play'd,

The an - gel of the Lord came down, And glo - ry shone a - round, And glo - ry shone a - round.
Glad ti - dings of great joy I bring To you and all man-kind, To you and all man-kind.
The Sav - ior who is Christ the Lord; And this shall be the sign, And this shall be the sign.
All mean-ly wrapp'd in swath-ing bands, And in a man-ger laid, And in a man-ger laid."

CHRISTIANS AWAKE,
SALUTE THE HAPPY MORN

Words by
JOHN BYROM

Music by
JOHN WAINWRIGHT

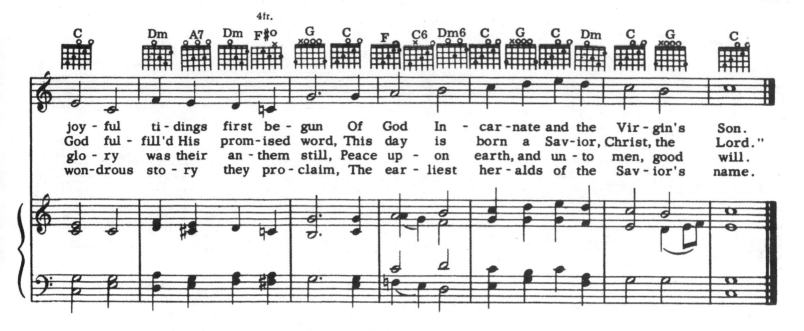

joy - ful ti - dings first be - gun Of God In - car - nate and the Vir - gin's Son.
God ful - fill'd His prom - ised word, This day is born a Sav - ior, Christ, the Lord."
glo - ry was their an - them still, Peace up - on earth, and un - to men, good will.
won - drous sto - ry they pro - claim, The ear - liest her - alds of the Sav - ior's name.

CAROL, SWEETLY CAROL

Words by
FRANCES J. Van ALSTYNE

Music by
T.E. PERKINS

1. Car - ol, sweet - ly car - ol, A Sav - iour born to -
2. Car - ol, sweet - ly car - ol, As when the an - gel
3. Car - ol, sweet - ly car - ol, The hap - py Christ - mas

day;___ Bear the joy - ful ti - dings, O, bear them far a - way!___
throng___ O'er the vales_ of Ju - dah, A - woke the heav'n - ly song;_
time;___ Hark! the bells_ are peal - ing Their mer - ry, mer - ry chime:_

INFANT SO GENTLE

Gascon Carol

WHAT MONTH WAS JESUS BORN IN?
(The Last Month of the Year)

Words and Music by
VERA HALL

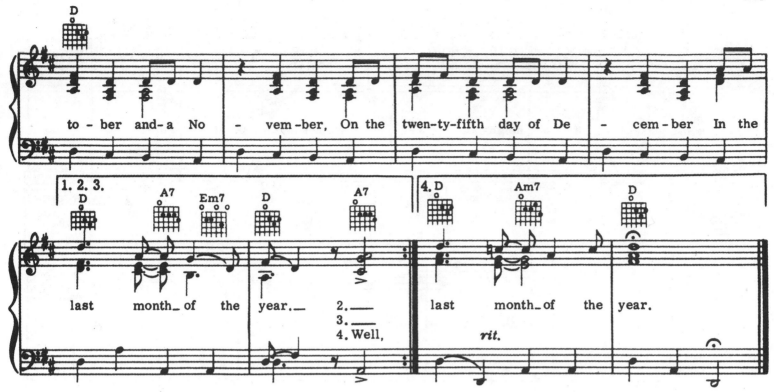

2. Well, they laid Him in the manger, Last month of the year! (2)
   (Chorus)
3. Wrapped Him up in swaddling clothes, Last month of the year! (2)
   (Chorus)
4. He was born of the Virgin Mary, Last month of the year! (2)
   (Chorus)

THE WONDERFUL WORLD OF CHRISTMAS

Words by
CHARLES TOBIAS

Music by
AL FRISCH

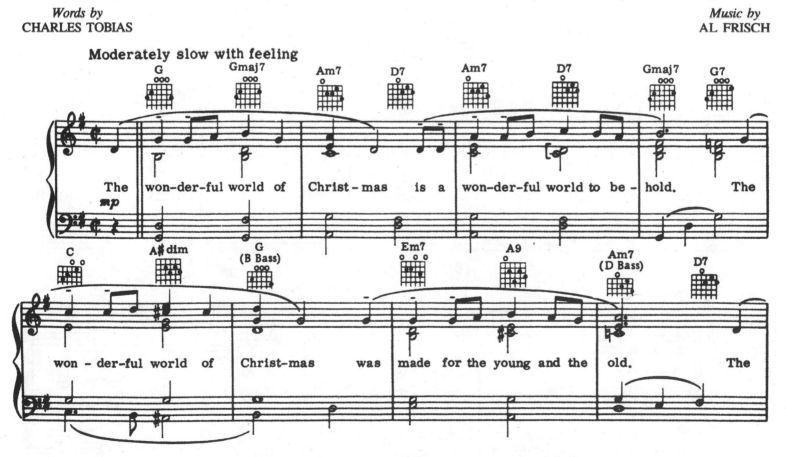

SILVER AND GOLD

Words and Music by
JOHNNY MARKS

Slowly and expressively

JINGLE, JINGLE, JINGLE

Words and Music by
JOHNNY MARKS

WHEN SANTA CLAUS GETS YOUR LETTER

Words and Music by
JOHNNY MARKS

THE MOST WONDERFUL DAY OF THE YEAR

Words and Music by
JOHNNY MARKS

JOYOUS CHRISTMAS

Words and Music by
JOHNNY MARKS

THE NIGHT BEFORE CHRISTMAS SONG

Words Adapted by
JOHNNY MARKS
From Clement Moore's Poem

Music by
JOHNNY MARKS

'Twas the night be - fore Christ - mas and all thru the house, not a
(And so) up to the house - top the rein - deer soon flew, with the

crea - ture was stir - ring not e - ven a mouse. All the
sleigh full of toys and Saint Nich - o - las too. Down the

stock - ings were hung by the chim - ney with care. In the
chim - ney he came with a leap and with a bound. He was

hope that Saint Nich - o - las soon would be there. Then
dressed all in fur and his bel - ly was round. He

CHRISTMAS CANDLES

Words and Music by
D. KAY, V. O'DEA
and JAY CLINTON

1. They say it's true of Christ-mas time, When fond ones are a - part, That
2. And I will make my Christ-mas wish A - lone by can-dle-light, And

if you wish by can-dle-light And love is in your heart, Your
pray the mes-sage that I send, Will find my love to - night. So

love will send a mag - ic light Up to the Christ-mas star. And
if your heart will nev - er stray Just tell the Christ-mas star. And

A-CAROLING WE GO

Words and Music by
JOHNNY MARKS

Moderately bright

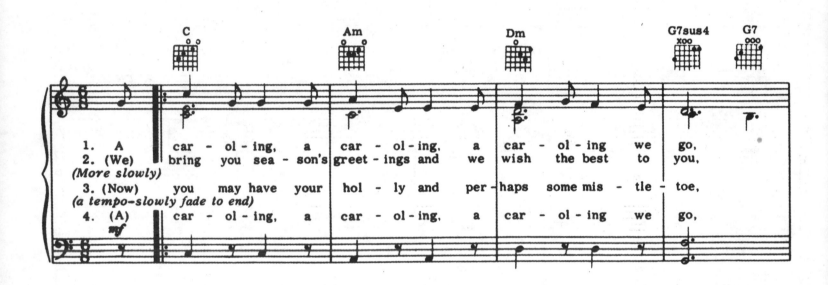

1. A car - ol - ing, a car - ol - ing, a car - ol - ing we go,
2. (We) bring you sea - son's greet - ings and we wish the best to you,
(More slowly)
3. (Now) you may have your hol - ly and per - haps some mis - tle - toe,
(a tempo-slowly fade to end)
4. (A) car - ol - ing, a car - ol - ing, a car - ol - ing we go,

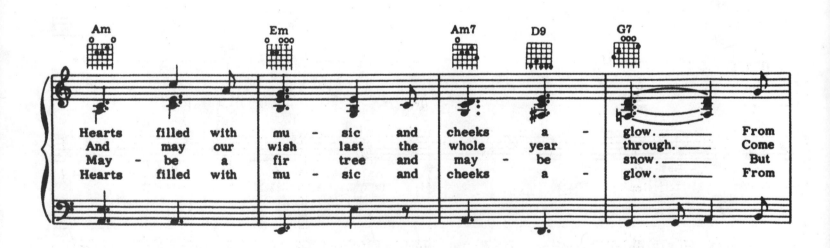

Hearts filled with mu - sic and cheeks a - glow. _____ From
And may our wish last the whole year through. _____ Come
May - be a fir tree and may - be snow. _____ But
Hearts filled with mu - sic and cheeks a - glow. _____ From

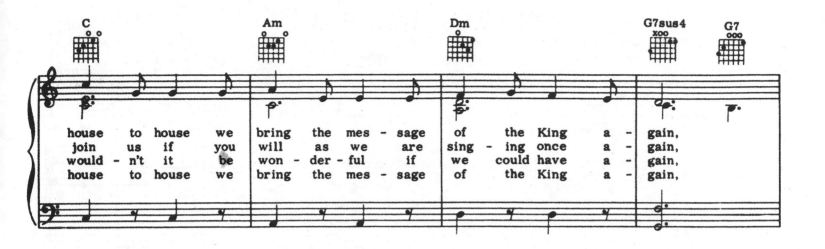

house to house we bring the mes - sage of the King a - gain,
join us if you will as we are sing - ing once a - gain,
would - n't it be won - der - ful if we could have a - gain,
house to house we bring the mes - sage of the King a - gain,

Peace On ___ Earth, Good Will To Men, Peace On ___ Earth, Good

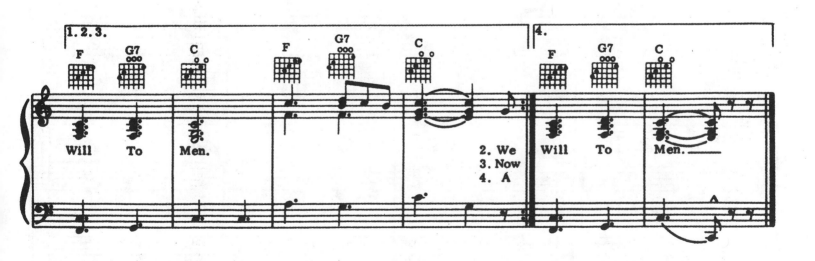

1. 2. 3.

Will To Men.

2. We
3. Now
4. A

4.

Will To Men. ___

CHRISTMAS MEM'RIES

Words by
ALAN and MARILYN BERGMAN

Music by
DON COSTA

MISTLETOE AND HOLLY

Words and Music by
FRANK SINATRA, DOK STANFORD
and HENRY SANICOLA

AMAZING GRACE

By
JOHN NEWTON
Early American Melody

THE FRIENDLY BEASTS

English XII Century
Arranged by J.C.

THE HOLLY AND THE IVY

Traditional Old French

1. The hol-ly and the i-vy, Now both are full well grown, Of
2. The hol-ly bears a blos-som As white as lil-y flow'r: And

all the trees that are in the wood, The hol-ly bears the crown.
Ma-ry bore sweet Je-sus Christ, To be our sweet Sav-ior.

REFRAIN

O the ris-ing of the sun, The run-ning of the deer, The play-ing of the

mer-ry or-gan, Sweet sing-ing in the quire, Sweet sing-ing in the quire.

BRING A TORCH, JEANNETTE, ISABELLA

Allegro

Traditional Provencal

1. Bring a torch,— Jean - nette, Is - a - bel - la! Bring a torch, to the cra - dle run! It is Je - sus, good folk of the vil - lage; Christ_ is born and Ma - ry's call - ing, Ah! ah! beau-ti-ful is the moth - er; Ah! ah! beau-ti - ful is her Son.___

2. It is wrong when the child — is sleep - ing, It is wrong_ to talk_ so loud; Si - lence, all, as you gath - er a - round,_ Lest_ your noise should wak - en Je - sus: Hush! hush! see — how fast He slum - bers; Hush! ah! hush! see — how fast He sleeps!___

HAIL TO THE LORD'S ANOINTED

Words by
JAMES MONTGOMERY

Music by
L. Van BEETHOVEN
from "Ninth Symphony"

COMES NOW, GOD'S BELOVED SON

By
J.S. BACH
English Version by
F.C.W.

1. Comes now God's be - lov - ed Son, Sav - iour, heav'ns ap - point - ed one,
2. Comes he now this day a Child, Off - spring of a Vir - gin mild,
3. Thru the years His pre - cepts stand, Con - stant, strong on ev - 'ry hand,

To re - deem us from our sins. Here as man He comes with man to dwell.
Comes to teach man - kind to make Full a - mends for faults and fol - lies done,
Will - ing hearts at His com - mand. When at last our life shall come to rest,

Earth - ly wrongs by grace to quell. We by faith, His works to tell.
By His love and truth di - vine, God's e - ter - nal gift sub - lime.
Torn by sin in earth - ly test, Sav'd are we, His name con - fess'd.

BRIGHTEST AND BEST

By
REV. J.F. THRUPP

AN EVENING PRAYER

Words by
C.M. BATTERSBY

Music by
CHAS H. GABRIEL

2. If I have uttered idle words or vain,
   If I have turned aside from want or pain,
   Lest I offend some other thru the strain,
   Dear Lord, forgive.

3. If I have been perverse, or hard, or cold,
   If I have longed for shelter in the fold,
   When Thou hast given me some fort to hold,
   Dear Lord, forgive.

4. Forgive the sins I have confessed to Thee;
   Forgive the secret sins I do not see;
   O guide me, love me, and my keeper be.
   Amen.

CHRISTMAS MORN IS COME AGAIN

Text Adapted

Slovak Carol
Arranged by F.C.W.

1. Christ-mas morn is come a-gain, Mer-ry church bells loud-ly ring,
2. Christ-mas morn is come a-gain, Shep-herds plod their wea-ry way,
3. Christ-mas morn is come a-gain, In-fant in a man-ger laid,

Christ-mas morn is come a-gain! Loud-ly hap-py chil-dren sing,
Christ-mas morn is come a-gain! At their feet the lamb-kins play.
Christ-mas morn is come a-gain! With His bless-ed Moth-er Maid,

"Glo-ry be to God on high" Re-sounds once more through
Three wise men from east-ern clime, Bring gifts all rich and
An-gels with their harps are nigh To sing their Mas-ter's

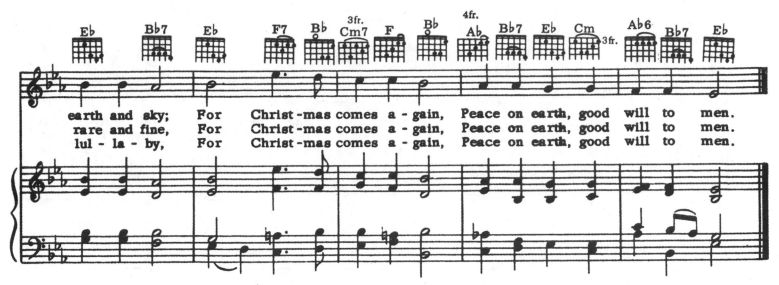

earth and sky; For Christ-mas comes a - gain, Peace on earth, good will to men.
rare and fine, For Christ-mas comes a - gain, Peace on earth, good will to men.
lul - la - by, For Christ-mas comes a - gain, Peace on earth, good will to men.

SONGS OF PRAISE THE ANGELS SANG

Words by
JAMES MONTGOMERY

Music by
ISAAC SMITH

1. Songs of praise the an - gels sang, Heav'n with Al - le -
2. Songs of praise a - woke the morn When the Prince of
3. Heav'n and earth must pass a - way; Songs of praise shall

lu - ias rang, When Je - ho - vah's work be - gun, When He spake and it was done.
Peace was born, Songs of praise a - rose when He, Cap - tive, led cap - tiv - i - ty.
crown that day: God will make new heav'ns and earth, Songs of praise shall hail their birth.

SONG OF THE SHIP

From a German MS - 1480
Andernach Gesangbuch, 1608

AS JOSEPH WAS A-WALKING
(Cherry Tree Carol)

Traditional English

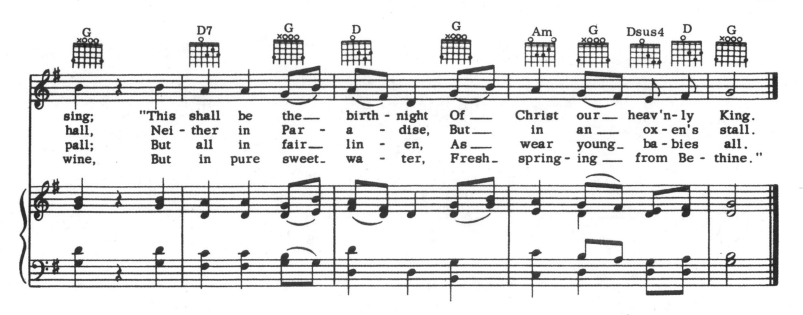

sing; "This shall be the— birth-night Of — Christ our— heav'n-ly King.
hall, Nei - ther in Par - a - dise, But— in an — ox-en's stall.
pall; But all in fair - lin - en, As — wear young— ba-bies all.
wine, But in pure sweet— wa - ter, Fresh— spring-ing — from Be - thine."

LITTLE CHILDREN, CAN YOU TELL?

Anonymous

Moderately,

1. Lit - tle chil - dren, can you tell? Do you know the sto - ry well, Ev - 'ry girl and
2. Yes, we know the sto - ry well; Lis - ten now, and hear us tell, Ev - 'ry girl and
3. For a lit - tle Babe that day, Cra - dled in a man - ger lay, Born on earth our

ev - 'ry boy, Why the an - gels sing for joy On the Christ-mas morn - ing.
ev - 'ry boy, Why the an - gels sing for joy On the Christ-mas morn - ing.
Lord to be, This the won-d'ring an-gels see On the Christ-mas morn - ing.

THE BIRTHDAY OF A KING

By
WILLIAM H. NEIDLINGER

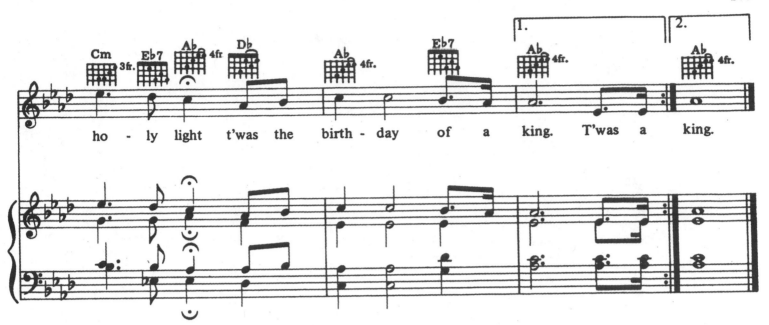

ho - ly light t'was the birth-day of a king. T'was a king.

THE BELLS OF PARADISE

Traditional English

1. What are those bells that chime so clear, O'er leaf-less trees and hill-top drear? They
2. What are those bells that chime so proud, Like an-gels chant-ing from a cloud? They
3. What are those bells that chime so far, Like ma-tins rung from star to star? They

are the bells of Par-a-dise, For to guide the sweet In-fant o'er snow and ice.
are the bells of Par-a-dise. He did come for a lamb and a sac-ri-fice.
are the bells of Par-a-dise, And His Moth-er did weep at the bit-ter price.

THE THREE KINGS

Flemish Carol

THE BOAR'S HEAD CAROL

Ancient Oxford Carol
XVI Century

CHORUS

Poco pesante

quick - ly drew near, Drums sound - ed their march as they quick - ly drew near.
Maid in her tears, So Jo - seph did com - fort the Maid in her tears.
life at a word, Such ten - der lambs robb'd of dear life at a word.

Ca - put a - pri de - fe - ro, Red - dens lau - des Do - mi - no!

Last time Fine

1. The boar's head, in hand bear I Be - deck'd with bays and rose - ma - ry. And I
2. The boar's head, I un - der - stand, The fin - est dish in all the land. Which is

Repeat chorus after second verse.

pray you mas - ters mer - ry be Qui est - is in con - viv - i - o.
thus be - deck'd with gay gar - land, Let us ser - vi - re can - ti - co.

Repeat chorus after second verse.

JOSEPH, O DEAR JOSEPH, MINE

XIV Century German
Based on the
"Resonet in Laudibus"

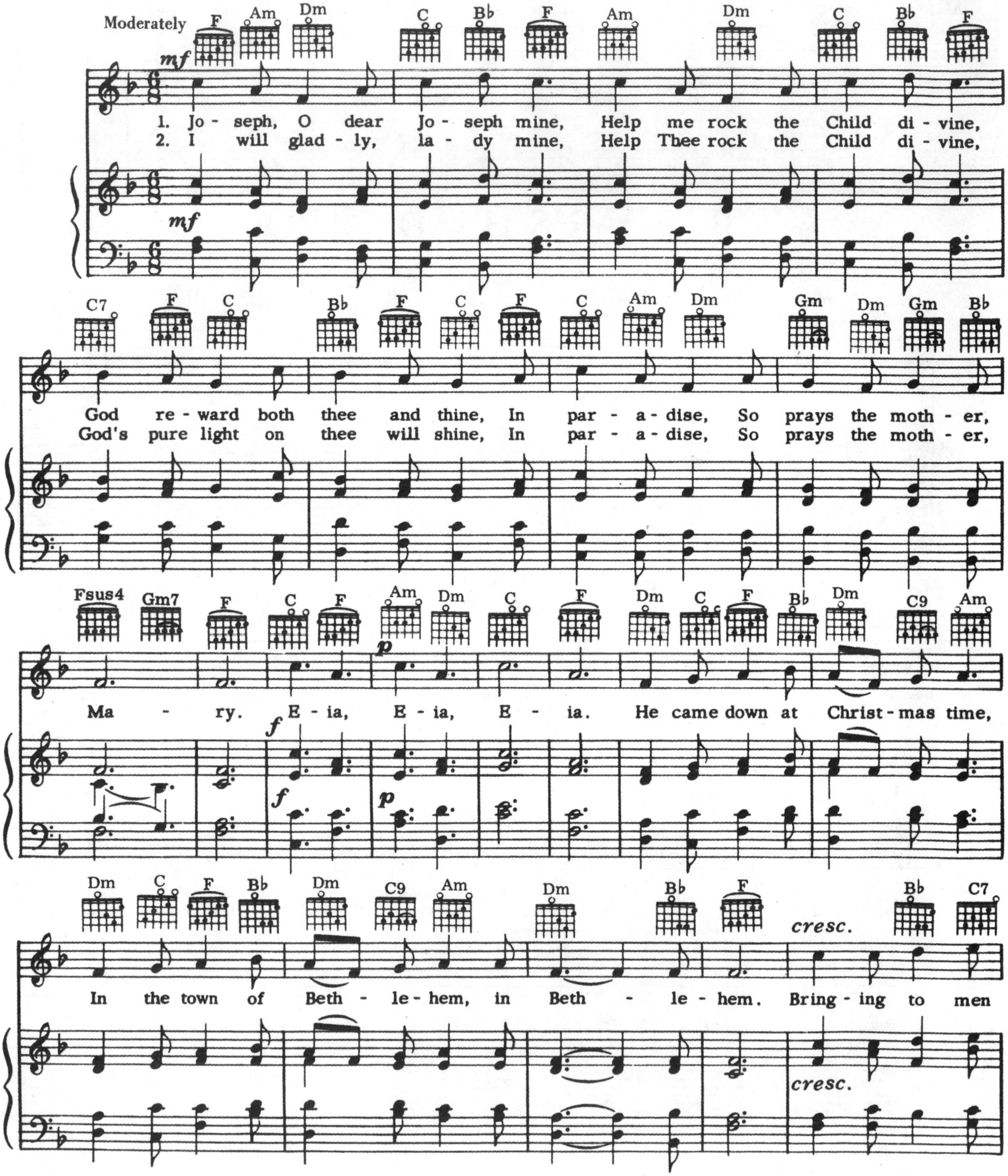

Moderately
F Am Dm C B♭ F Am Dm C B♭ F
mf
1. Jo - seph, O dear Jo - seph mine, Help me rock the Child di - vine,
2. I will glad - ly, la - dy mine, Help Thee rock the Child di - vine,
C7 F C B♭ F C F C Am Dm Gm Dm Gm B♭
God re - ward both thee and thine, In par - a - dise, So prays the moth - er,
God's pure light on thee will shine, In par - a - dise, So prays the moth - er,
Fsus4 Gm7 F C F Am Dm C F Dm C F B♭ Dm C9 Am
p
f
Ma - ry. E - ia, E - ia, E - ia. He came down at Christ - mas time,
Dm C F B♭ Dm C9 Am Dm B♭ F B♭ C7
cresc.
In the town of Beth - le - hem, in Beth - le - hem. Bring - ing to men

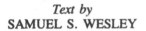

far and wide, Love's di - a - dem, E - ia, E - ia Lull - a - by.

O HARK! WHAT MEAN THOSE HOLY VOICES

Text by
SAMUEL S. WESLEY

French Noel
Arranged by
DOUGLAS MacLEAN

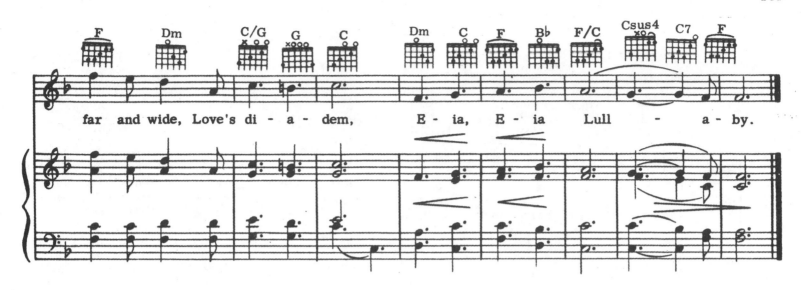

1. O hark, what mean those ho - ly voic - es Sweet-ly sound-ing thro' the skies?
2. Come lis - ten to the won-drous sto - ry, Which they sing in hymns of joy,
3. For Christ is born, the great A - noint - ed! Heav'n and earth his prais - es sing!

Lo!_ th'an-gel - ic host_ re-joic - es, Heav'n-ly Al - le - lu - ias rise.
"Glo - ry in the high-est, glo - ry, Glo - ry be_ to God most high".
O _ re-ceive whom God_ ap-point - ed For your Pro - phet, Priest and King!

SING WE NOËL

French Carol

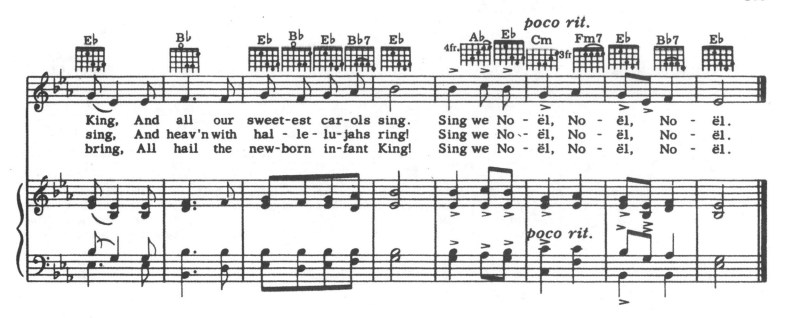

King, And all our sweet-est car-ols sing. Sing we No - ël, No - ël, No - ël.
sing, And heav'n with hal - le - lu-jahs ring! Sing we No - ël, No - ël, No - ël.
bring, All hail the new-born in-fant King! Sing we No - ël, No - ël, No - ël.

AS EACH HAPPY CHRISTMAS

1. As each hap - py Christ - mas Dawns on earth a -
2. En - ters with His bless - ing In - to ev - 'ry
3. All un - known, be - side me He will ev - er

gain, Comes the ho - ly Christ - child To the hearts of men.
home, Guides and guards our foot - steps As we go and come.
stand, And will safe - ly lead me With his own right hand.

FROM EVERY SPIRE ON CHRISTMAS EVE

Words by
ELEANOR A. HUNTER

Music by
GEORGE COLES

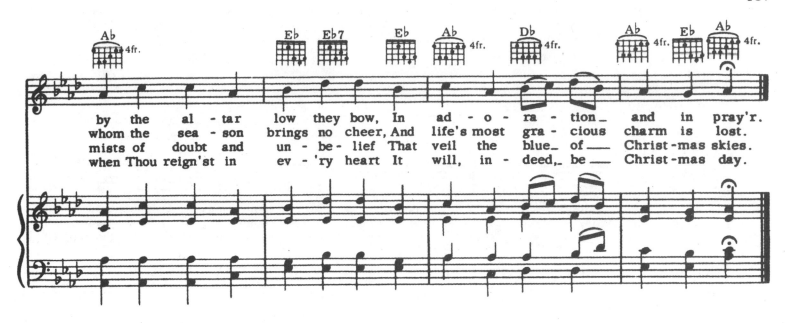

by the al - tar low they bow, In ad - o - ra - tion_ and in pray'r.
whom the sea - son brings no cheer, And life's most gra - cious charm is lost.
mists of doubt and un - be - lief That veil the blue_ of __ Christ-mas skies.
when Thou reign'st in ev - 'ry heart It will, in - deed,_ be __ Christ-mas day.

I SAW THREE SHIPS

Traditional English
XV Century Legend

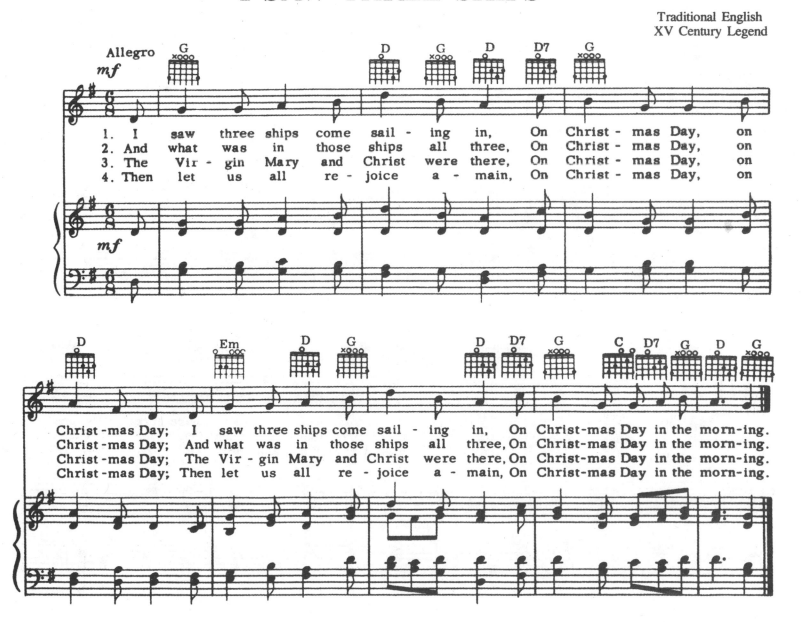

1. I saw three ships come sail - ing in, On Christ - mas Day, on
2. And what was in those ships all three, On Christ - mas Day, on
3. The Vir - gin Mary and Christ were there, On Christ - mas Day, on
4. Then let us all re - joice a - main, On Christ - mas Day, on

Christ-mas Day; I saw three ships come sail - ing in, On Christ-mas Day in the morn-ing.
Christ-mas Day; And what was in those ships all three, On Christ-mas Day in the morn-ing.
Christ-mas Day; The Vir - gin Mary and Christ were there, On Christ-mas Day in the morn-ing.
Christ-mas Day; Then let us all re - joice a - main, On Christ-mas Day in the morn-ing.

REMEMBER, O THOU MAN

By
THOMAS RAVENSCROFT

BEAUTIFUL SAVIOUR
(Crusader's Hymn)

Traditional

OH, HOW JOYFULLY
(O Sanctissima)

Words by
J. FALK

Sicilian Hymn

Allegretto

1. Oh, how joy-ful-ly___ Oh, how mer-ri-ly___ Christ-mas
2. Oh, how joy-ful-ly___ Oh, how mer-ri-ly___ Christ-mas
3. Oh, how joy-ful-ly___ Oh, how mer-ri-ly___ Christ-mas

comes with its grace di - vine! Grace a - gain is beam - ing,
comes with its peace di - vine! Peace on earth is reign - ing,
comes with its life di - vine! An - gels high in glo - ry,

Christ the world re - deem - ing Hail, ye Chris - tians, hail the joy-ous Christ-mas time!
Christ our peace re - gain - ing Hail, ye Chris - tians, hail the joy-ous Christ-mas time!
Chant the Christ-mas sto - ry: Hail, ye Chris - tians, hail the joy-ous Christ-mas time!

PAT-A-PAN

Burgundian, 17th Century

WASSAIL, WASSAIL!

Traditional